THE POWER PAMPHLET

THE POWER PAMPHLET

A Tool Box For Maximization

DORION D. MILLS

$Money Maid

Dorion D. Mills
The Power Pamphlet

Published by Spines
ISBN: 978-965-578-981-2

Contents

Introduction

> "This is my handwritten promise & declaration to you that this, *The Power Pamphlet*, was written & constructed with the full intent & purpose of being as influential & empowering to its readers as can be.
>
> **- Dorion D. Mills**

Letter

For the most part, I have yet to be blessed with the pleasure of meeting you in person. As much as I would have enjoyed giving you your copy of *The Power Pamphlet* personally, unfortunately I could not.

Until the time does present itself when we can gift one another with each other's presence, may you be enveloped in truth & greatness be upon you.

"Giving people back the power they never knew they possessed."

- Miguel "Logan" Hernandez

One

The ONLY thing harder than TRUST is BELIEF.

Two

EVERYDAY is filled with an assortment of options & offers between RIGHT NOW & FOREVER.

Three

You AREN'T doing what you should be doing when you're NOT doing what certain people WANT or EXPECT of you.

Four

HONESTY needs no belief or justification.

Five

Use YESTERDAY to get you through TODAY, & NOW to help you look forward to TOMORROW.

Six

The opposite of LOVE is DISREGARD.

Seven

PARENTS, don't forget to be FRIENDS.

Eight

Children LISTEN to their parents, they TALK to their friends.

Nine

IGNORANT people's worries are seldom.

Ten

INTELLIGENT people's worries are few.

Eleven

There will NEVER be another RIGHT NOW!

Twelve

ADJUST your reception.

Thirteen

TOO MUCH & NOT ENOUGH make PRIDE & DIGNITY look alike.

Fourteen

Every person has three people in their life:

- *The One* they want
- *The One* who wants them
- *The One* they have.

When you've found *The One* who is all three, you've found "LOVE."

Fifteen

The giver should never remember.

Sixteen

The receiver should never forget.

Seventeen

Watch out for people who ask for your last, like, the people who give their last watch out for you.

Eighteen

The word STYLE begins w/a YOU.

Nineteen

There is exclusivity in, “NO.”

Twenty

Beware of beliefs.

Twenty-one

There is no yesterday w/out today & there will be no tomorrow w/out NOW.

Twenty-two

T-R-U-S-T, you can't spell TRUST without a YOU and a ME.

Twenty-three

A mother's son is NEVER GUILTY.

Twenty-four

A father's daughter is ALWAYS INNOCENT.

Twenty-five

Wealth without understanding is WORTHLESS.

Twenty-six

BEWARE, for some gifts are INVESTMENTS.

Twenty-seven

Doing something ALWAYS does something.

Twenty-eight

Accountability speaks louder for maturity than age does.

Twenty-nine

Doing what you want to do & doing what needs to be done is the difference between a man and a boy.

Thirty

BEST is an abbreviation for BETTER THAN THE REST.

Thirty-one

Do what you're SUPPOSED to do & you will NEVER do what you "HAVE TO."

Thirty-two

WORK washes wishes away.

Thirty-three

You CANNOT live in the past & look forward to the future.

Thirty-four

Fishing poles or fish sticks?

Thirty-five

The world is NOT yours, but IT DOES revolve around you.

Thirty-six

Don't let knowledge make you ignorant.

Thirty-seven

Familiarity is influential in understanding.

Thirty-eight

You don’t have to say “SORRY” when you apologize.

Thirty-nine

DO what you want to do & it will be a challenge to BE what you want to be.

Forty

Math with letters is poetry.

Forty-one

DETAILS are seldom, but HIGHLY appreciated.

Forty-two

If you can't read, learn to count well.

Forty-three

What you have & how you treat it, is a reflection of what you want & if you deserve it.

Forty-four

THOUGHTS motivate you; FEELINGS move you.

Forty-five

Leave something to come back to.

Forty-six

EVERYONE wants to hear what the person who hasn't said anything has to say.

Forty-seven

There is no such thing as RESPONSIBILITY without sacrifice.

Forty-eight

People not loving you back is NOT the equivalent of nobody loving you.

Forty-nine

You're known for what you DO, remembered for what you DID.

Fifty

Relationships are worth more than money.

Fifty-one

Don't let the way a person feels about themself come between you & how you feel about yourself.

Fifty-two

The past is a place you visit, NOT reside.

Fifty-three

Dreams are for BELIEVERS, nightmares for the DOUBTFUL.

Fifty-four

One “NO”, can erase one million “YES’.”

Fifty-five

Self-control is a form of loyalty.

Fifty-six

Nothing is harder to hide than the feelings you have for something you DON'T WANT TO care about.

Fifty-seven

You're better than NO ONE, but who is equal to you?

Fifty-eight

Don't let what someone does for you be the only thing that gets DONE for you.

Fifty-nine

TRUST enables you to DO great things, BELIEF allows you to WITNESS them.

Sixty

Smiles are contagious.

Sixty-one

Too many OPINIONS can turn a DECISION into a DEBATE.

Sixty-two

CONFRONTATION has a nemesis; its name is COMMUNICATION.

Sixty-three

The ONLY thing BETTER than YOU is a BETTER YOU.

Sixty-four

HAPPINESS & JOY are two different words, but PEACE brings both.

Sixty-five

HONESTY will get you more of what you want than LYING or stealing.

Sixty-six

A truth withheld is ALMOST A LIE.

Sixty-seven

The same thing that got you noticed can get you ignored.

Sixty-eight

Limitations are relative to dreams in the sense that, WHATEVER you think can happen, can actually happen.

Sixty-nine

Confidence for sons & self-esteem for daughters.

Seventy

NOTHING enters w/out your clearance.

Seventy-one

JEALOUSY wishes it was him, ENVY wishes it wasn't you.

Seventy-two

INTEREST is to be EARNED.

Seventy-three

A level of selfishness is REQUIRED in order for one to be considered "GENEROUS."

Seventy-four

Apologies & acceptance are OWED as much as compliments & should be appreciated as much.

Seventy-five

What you do, what you did & what you've done, ALL shine a light on one another.

Seventy-six

You react to what happens differently when you know why it happened.

Seventy-seven

There are two who are BRUTALLY honest: those who TRULY have love for you & those who TRULY don't.

Seventy-eight

Take all your chances & trade them in for risks.

Seventy-nine

Count on time to fly.

Eighty

WHAT happened or WHY it happened, speaks volumes for the person who wants to know.

Eighty-one

Careful of what you care about.

Eighty-two

You CANNOT outrun a problem.

Eighty-three

Use the past for guidance, knowledge for direction & the future for fuel.

Eighty-four

LIABILITY: A continuous loss that you STILL haven't learned from.

Eighty-five

Fear is a tool, but it doesn't work on everyone.

Eighty-six

May all of your prayers be spelled WITHOUT an "E."

Eighty-seven

The coward is slave to the aggressor, as is, the aggressor to the wise.

Eighty-eight

Love is NOT always served with desert.

Eight-nine

Do SOME things & you will do ANYTHING.

Ninety

WEALTH is OPTIONS; more of it, more of them.

Ninety-one

One of the 2 differences between FRIENDS and FAMILY is the spelling.

Ninety-two

Let NO ONE find routine in what you find uncomfortable.

Ninety-three

Both PERCEPTION & SUSPICION are prisons that only reality can release you from.

Ninety-four

Suspicions NOT extinguished, become delusional fires.

Ninety-five

The influential aren't easily influenced.

Ninety-six

FEW who see you walking know where you're coming from,
LESS than that know where you're going?

Ninety-seven

It is just as difficult to stop a bad thing as it is to start a good thing.

Ninety-eight

You can get a lot accomplished by sitting still.

Ninety-nine

Things CHANGE: If you took the CREDIT, take the BLAME.

One hundred

Both, “IM SORRY” & “I LOVE YOU”, look better than they sound.

One hundred and one

And then what?

One hundred and two

BEGGARS & BULLETS: Two things NOBODY wants to see coming their way.

One hundred and three

PEACE isn't as important as PROTOCOL.

One hundred and four

A TALENT is a gift meant to be shared.

One hundred and five

TIME & TECHNOLOGY: both, NEVER stop or go in REVERSE.

One hundred and six

NEVER let a person who ISN'T speak on behalf of those who ARE.

One hundred and seven

Appreciation should be appreciated.

One hundred and eight

If you DO NOT control yourself, something or someone else WILL.

One hundred and nine

DON'T forget about YOU.

One hundred and ten

Put the "same type" of people together, and you will see how DIFFERENT people are

One hundred and eleven

Politics make business unfair.

One hundred and twelve

Your FEARS reside in a house that you built.

One hundred and thirteen

Too much talk about things you know nothing about, eventually you will be asked to do something you don't know how to do.

One hundred and fourteen

BELIEF doesn't work w/out TRUST and this is how FAITH operates.

One hundred and fifteen

Patience(+ Obligation(+ Will(+ Entegrity(+ Responsibility = POWER

One hundred and sixteen

EASY to not LIKE people you don't know, HARD to not LOVE people you do.

One hundred and seventeen

A person seeking ventilation needs no advice.

One hundred and eighteen

DECISIONS can be split, but CHOICES LAST A LIFETIME.

One hundred and nineteen

Take advantage NOT for granted.

One hundred and twenty

Elders for information, adolescents for updates.

One hundred and twenty-one

SUPPORT is NOT always convenient.

This is dedicated to EVERYONE, EVERYWHERE &
EVERYTHING that EVER, told me, showed or made me feel like
I wasn't enough.
I NEVER took it personally, I ALWAYS went back to the drawing
board & always got good or better.
And for that you are appreciated.

"The Goal is to leave people better that you found them."
- Tommie "Baser" McDaniel.

$ Money Maid

www.ingramcontent.com/pod-product-compliance
Lightning Source LLC
LaVergne TN
LVHW090936150826
845672LV00006B/1533

* 9 7 8 9 6 5 5 7 8 9 8 1 2 *